"EL TORO MANOLITO"

" The Bull Manolito"

Autor.- **Miguel Estaña**

"EL PINTOR DE INTERNET"

http://www.elpintordeinternet.com

Para realizar pedidos de este libro, contacte con:
Palibrio
1663 Liberty Drive
Suite 200
Bloomington, IN 47403
Gratis desde EE. UU. al 877.407.5847
Gratis desde México al 01.800.288.2243
Gratis desde España al 900.866.949
Desde otro país al +1.812.671.9757
Fax: 01.812.355.1576
ventas@palibrio.com
[433152]

"EL TORO MANOLITO"

" The Bull Manolito"

Autor.- **Miguel Estaña**

"EL PINTOR DE INTERNET"

http://www.elpintordeinternet.com

L don ̈t know what has happened to our son?

Me neighter

Son! Why don´t you eat?

L¨m not hungry

3

L´think I know what has happened to him

His cousin might have toid him a story

L hope he didn¨t tell him the truth

lf he did , he won¨t feel like playing anymore

¡Papa!, ¡Papa! , are you happy?

Ofcourse 1 am,why you want to know?

Do you think he found out?

It¨s possible, because he looks sad and he doesn¨t play with his friends.

Son, I have to tell you something, we are going on a trip, very far. And it will take some time before we get back.

I don´t want you to go!

One day you will understand my son

They offer all the bulls at the age of four a free trip It´s very kind of these animals that walk on two legs,

Pasaron tres años

¿Que extraño que no vengan mis padres

Three years have passed

How strange that my parents don´t return

How great,soon I will see my parents   Go! Go!   -One   way   trip-

¡Papa! I´m here!

¡¡Que lugar más raro !!

¡¡ What a strange place !!

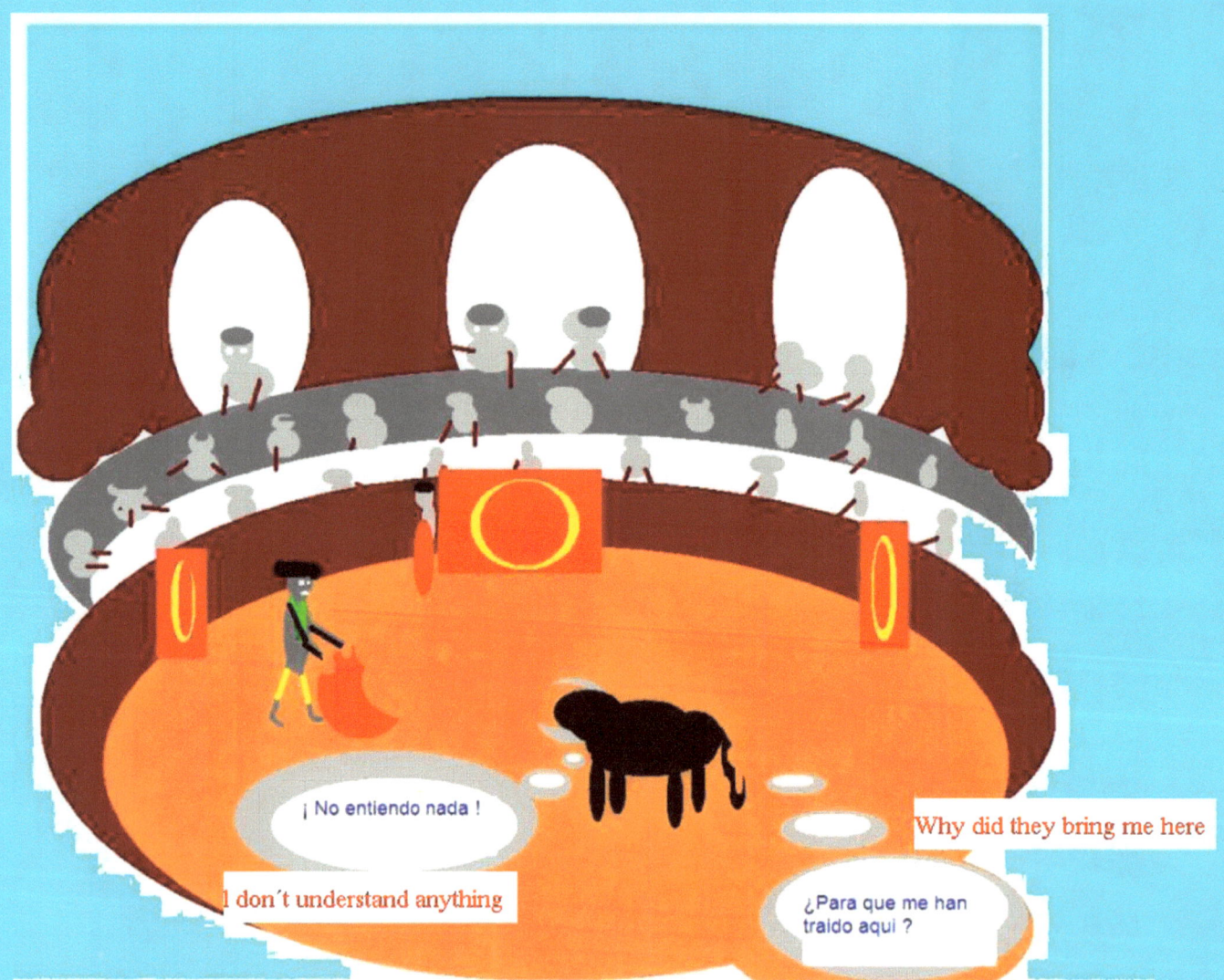

14

After getting high, manipulate and torture me, leave me dead

Despues de drogarme, manipularme y torturarma, me dejan con vida.

15

Plaza de Toros

Bullring

¡Que horrible ha sido la tortura! y como se han divertido estos desalmados.

That horrible has been the torture! And since cruel these have amused themselves!.

They tear the thick darts our of my skith with meat on it-Wat a terrible pain!

No han tenido compasión y se han divertido mucho.

They didn´t feel sorry about it, quite the opposite. They had a good time!